Table of Contents

Color Chart and Supply List

Artist Paints

Liquitex Acrylics	**Ceramcoat**
AR/Acra Red	————
BS/Burnt Sienna	Burnt Sienna
BU/Burnt Umber	Burnt Umber
CYM/Cadmium Yellow Medium	Bright Yellow
CoB/Colbalt Blue	Ultra Blue
DP/Dioxazine Purple	Purple
HG/Hookers Green	Deep River
NC/Naphthol Crimson	Naphthol Crimson
PhB/Phthalocyanine Blue	Phthalo Blue
PhG/Phthalocyanine Green	Phthalo Green
PyG/Paynes Gray	Black
RO/Red Oxide	Georgia Clay
RS/Raw Sienna	Raw Sienna
UmB/Ultramarine Blue	Navy
YO/Yellow Oxide	Straw
W/Titanium White	White

(Velvet clothing may only be achieved with Liquitex pure pigment colors.)

Brushes
Liquitex #5 or #4 series 5000 Sable round Kolinsky Sable.
Variety of flat brushes.
Sponge brushes for basing and varnishing.

Sealer
Blair satin spray varnish

Base Paints
Carver Tripps Contempo Enamel — Burgundy
Ceramcoat — Ivory
Accent Country Colors — Pine Needle Green

Transferring Patterns
Transfer paper

Finishing Products
Blair Satin spray varnish and water base varnish.
Extra fine sand paper and steel wool.

General Instructions

1. **Preparations**
linen canvas — none
wood — seal with spray varnish, sand and base 2 coats of paint
wood cutouts — seal with spray varnish and sand (no base paint) with extra fine sand paper.
porcelain — none
glass — none (must be clean)
2. **Basing on Base Paint**
Apply paint with sponge brush and sand with extra fine steel wool between coats. Lighter colors may need more than 2 coats. Dry thoroughly before transferring pattern.
3. **Transferring patterns**
Place transfer paper chalky side down onto project. Put traced-off pattern on next and trace over design with stylus or pencil. Pattern may be taped down to prevent shifting while tracing. Excess markings may be cleaned off with 409 and paper towel.
4. **Paint on Design**
5. **Finishing**
Spray with Blair Satin varnish or brush on a water base varnish — many coats. Porcelain should be spray varnished so you don't wipe off your design. Glass should be varnished with a gloss over design only. (Don't use waterbase.)

Color Mixes
Burgundy Mix: 2 parts NC and 1 part DP
Green Mix: HG and PhG (equal parts)
Royal Blue Mix: UmB and DP (equal parts)
Turquoise Mix: 2 parts PhB and 1 part BU
Mauve Mix: 3 parts NC and 2 parts BU and 1 part DP plus White (lots of white for a pale mauve)
Dusty Purple Mix: 2 parts BU and 1 part DP
Pale Dusty Purple Mix: Same as above and lots of White
Kim Gold Mix: Add gold bronzing powder to Kim Gold (equal parts) for better and brighter coverage.

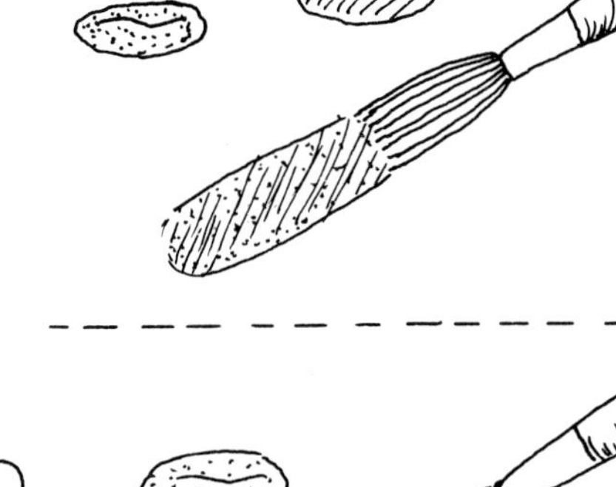

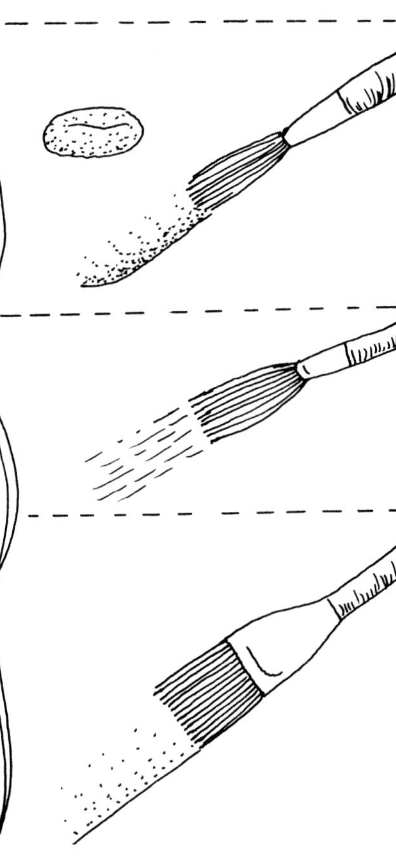

Wash: half water and half paint mixed together (should be transparent on project)
Double load side by side: dip one corner of the brush in one color of paint and the other corner in another color. To start the blending process pull on your pallete several times in the same spot causing the two colors to blend in the middle of the brush. You should still be able to see a clean edge of each color on the outer edges. Apply to surface by squishing down hard as you pull each stroke.
Thin lines: mix half paint and half water, load brush and twist on pallete wringing out all excess paint. If you get a line that skips in spots, there is not enough water in the mixture. If you get bubbles, there is not enough paint in your mixture. Hold your brush straight up and down barely letting the bristles touch.
Double load: fully loading brush with one color and picking up another either on the top or bottom side of the brush. Do not pre-mix the colors together on the pallete. Let the blending happen as you pull each stroke on the surface. Try not to restroke on the surface so you don't lose the pretty streaks of color.
Side load: load color onto only one side or corner of the brush and nothing on the other. Pull on your pallete removing any excess paint and starting the blending process so the when you pull your stroke it will go from color to nothing. There should not be a definite line on the side you did not have any paint.
Dry brush: use a completely dry brush, dip into paint and wipe several times on a paper towel causing the paint to come off the brush. Don't use much pressure when skimming across the surface of your project.
Floating color: dip brush into water, then set bristles on paper towel until the shinyness disappears. Dip one corner into paint and wipe on pallete several times causing the stroke to blend from color to nothing. There should be a definite edge on one side but not on the other. Sometimes you may want to moisten the surface first with water or extender so that you can pull a longer stroke.

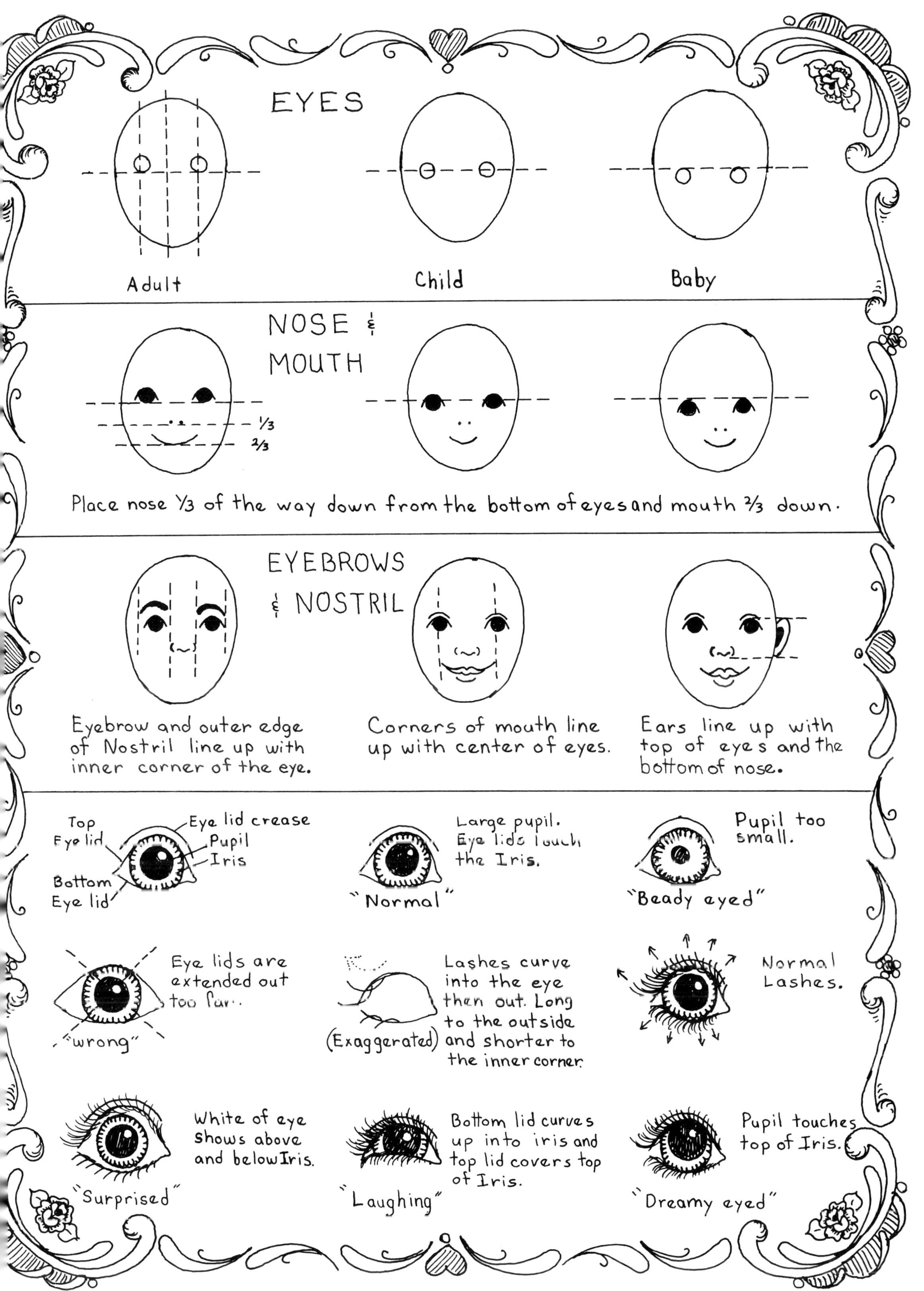

EYES
Adult
Child
Baby
NOSE & MOUTH
1/3
2/3
Place nose 1/3 of the way down from the bottom of eyes and mouth 2/3 down.
EYEBROWS & NOSTRIL
Eyebrow and outer edge of Nostril line up with inner corner of the eye.
Corners of mouth line up with center of eyes.
Ears line up with top of eyes and the bottom of nose.
Top Eye lid
Eye lid crease
Pupil
Iris
Bottom Eye lid
Large pupil. Eye lids touch the Iris.
"Normal"
Pupil too small.
"Beady eyed"
Eye lids are extended out too far.
"wrong"
(Exaggerated)
Lashes curve into the eye then out. Long to the outside and shorter to the inner corner.
Normal Lashes.
White of eye shows above and below Iris.
"Surprised"
Bottom lid curves up into iris and top lid covers top of Iris.
"Laughing"
Pupil touches top of Iris.
"Dreamy eyed"

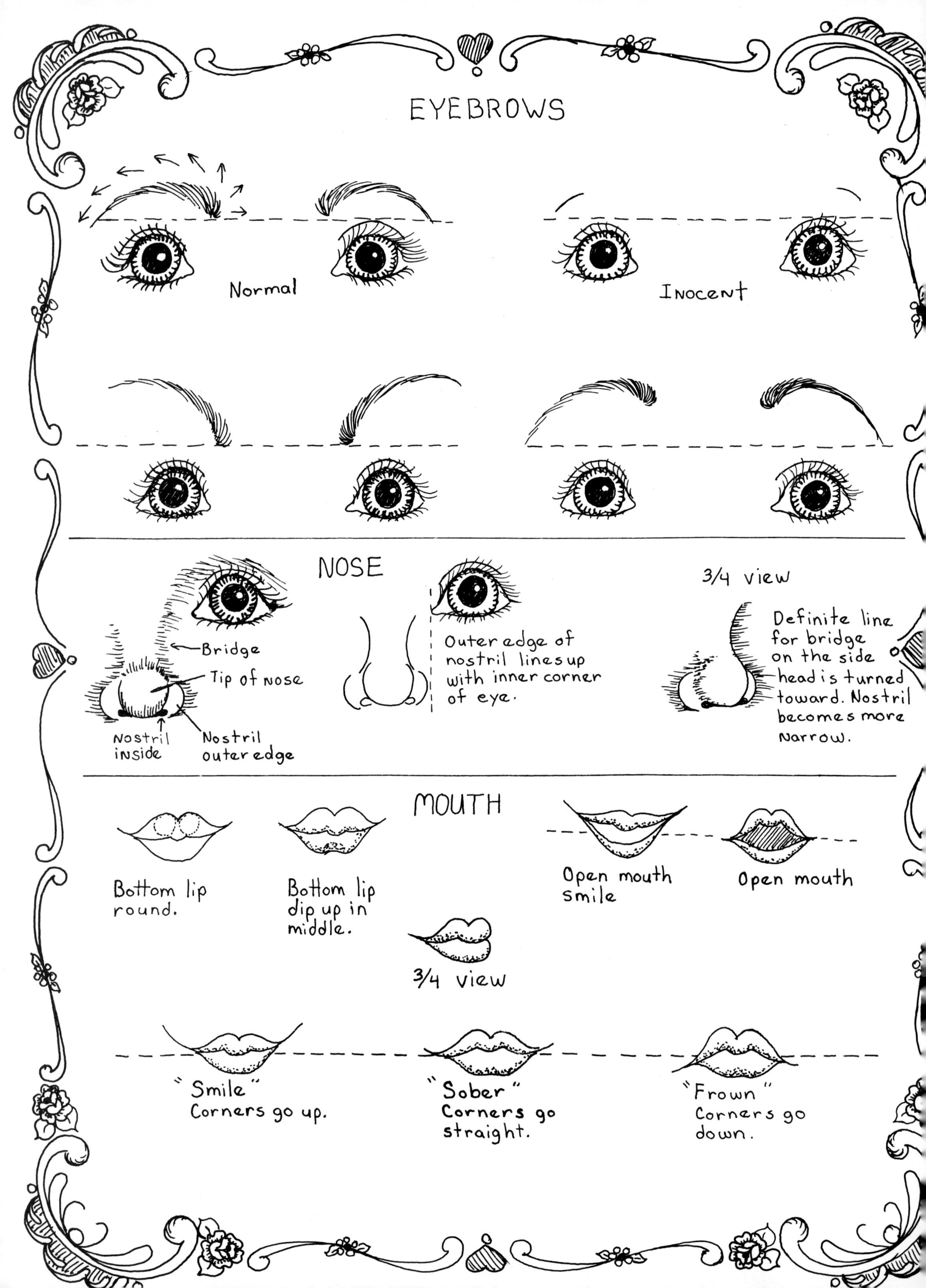
EYEBROWS
Normal
Inocent
NOSE
Bridge
Tip of nose
Nostril inside
Nostril outer edge
Outer edge of nostril lines up with inner corner of eye.
3/4 view
Definite line for bridge on the side head is turned toward. Nostril becomes more narrow.
MOUTH
Bottom lip round.
Bottom lip dip up in middle.
Open mouth smile
Open mouth
3/4 view
"Smile" Corners go up.
"Sober" Corners go straight.
"Frown" Corners go down.

General Face Instructions

Painting a Face Written in Order of Procedure

See page 14 for color Illustration.

Flesh Mix: 10 parts White and 1 part RO. (Add a touch of CYM for more of a golden tone). It's a good idea to pre-mix a whole jar of white — making it into flesh. Then you will always have the exact color with which to touch up.

Placing the Features: Free handing on the eyes, nose, and mouth may be done with a BS wash.

Preparation for Shading With Extender: Moisten the area to be shaded with "Folk Art Extender." On a small face the whole face may be moistened at the same time. On a very large face you may want to only moisten one section at a time. As long as the painted on features are dry you need not worry about brushing right over them with extender.

1. Proceed with extender by dipping brush into extender. The brush will appear shiny. Set it onto a paper towel until the shine disappears. Then moisten area to be shaded.

2. Clean brush in water and dab off on paper towel. Use largest brush you can handle for the size face you are working on. Load one corner of a flat brush with BS and blend several times on palette. Shade around hair line, behind eyes (above the crease line), down the sides of the nose, outside edges of nostrils, canal under nose, bottom tip of nose, above tip of nose and under lips.

Lip Mix: 2 parts AR and 1 part flesh mix. Fill in lips. Shade with BS the bottom of both lips. Highlight top of both lips with W.

Cheeks: are AR. Re-apply extender before putting on cheek color. Corner load AR onto flat brush and blend all excess paint off onto palette (paint should be very dry). With the color edge of brush up, pull from the nose down and around to the outside of the face. Quickly repeat but reverse brush with color side down and blend across the top of your first color. All color should be in the center of the cheek and fade off both directions with no sharp lines.

Blushing Accents: Use AR to also bring color throughout other areas of the face with a watered-down dry brush. Apply to the bottom of the chin and across the top of the forehead.

Eyes: (refer to step-by-step sample)

1. Outline iris with BU
2. Fill in with transparent wash of desired eye color — BS or BU for brown eyes, CoB for blue eyes, HG or PhG for green eyes.
3. Fill in pupil with PyG.
4. Place a W dot in the upper right hand corner of pupil.
5. On large faces only pull in little lines of iris color all around the inside edge of iris.
6. Lashes are BU (see examples as to directions). Mix paint with half water in order to get skinny lines. Sometimes you may want to omit the bottom lashes on a smaller face for a softer look.

Nose: may be outlined with BS on the outer edges of nostrils and connecting dots underneath. See example for where to shade.

Highlights: With a watered-down dry brush of W do the top of the chin, cheeks, and nose. Put an extra dot of white on the tip of nose and blot with your finger.

Hair Instructions

1. Fill in the entire area of hair with base color. It's OK if hair appears a little transparent. This just adds to the highlights.
2. Shading areas are indicated by ink lines on drawings (including tips of hair — thin lines). All areas that dip in need to be shaded.
3. First, highlight goes wherever the hair bumps out. This is indicated on pattern by the blank areas. Do not go all the way in the extreme edges that are shaded. Allow some of the base color to show through (thin lines).
4. Final highlight goes directly through the center portion of the first highlight. Be careful not to let this final highlight get into the shaded areas (thin lines).

Blonde:
Base: YO or YO and W (for pale blonde)
Shade: RS
First Highlight: YO and W (equal parts)
Final Highlight: W

Light Brown:
Base: RS
Shade: BU
First Highlight: RS and W
Final Highlight: RS and W (more white)

Dark Brown:
Base: BU (wash)
Shade: PyG
First Highlight: RS
Final Highlight: RS and W

Warm Brown:
Base: BS
Shade: BU
First Highlight: RS
Final Highlight: RS and W

Black:
Base: BU
Shade: PyG
First Highlight: BU and W
Final Highlight: BU and more W

Red:
Base: RO
Shade: BS or BU
First Highlight: RS
Final Highlight: RS and W

Helpful Hints

If you want hair darker, simply add more shading color; if a lighter color is desired, add more highlight lines. If you possibly made too many highlight or shading lines, simply make some more lines with original base color. Don't be afraid to experiment or re-stroke.

General Instructions for Velvet Clothes

(See page 20)

1. Base in area with desired color.
   A. Double load round brush with base color completely first, then side load with white.
   B. Blend on palette several times in the same spot.
   C. Be sure to have a definite base color on one side and white on the other for a very dramatic look. With W to the outer edge, squish down hard while pulling along edge and lift gradually towards the end. Don't be afraid to re-stroke if the first time didn't blend enough. You may also let it dry and try again if needed. The secret to rich velvet is loading the brush with globs of paint. Ridges in the paint strokes are just a part of the look.
   D. Create as many folds as desired, keeping W to the left on the left side of clothes and reversing in the middle so W will be to the right on the right side.
   E. Velvet that has been based with a very dark color needs no shading. Medium colors of velvet may be shaded on the underside of the folds. Use the same procedure as the W highlighting. Lots of contrast in color will create a dramatic dimensional look.

Green Velvet:
Green mix base
White highlights

Burgundy Velvet:
Burgundy mix base
White highlights
DP shading

Royal Blue Velvet:
Royal Blue mix base
White highlights

Turquoise Velvet:
Turquoise mix base
White highlights

Mauve Velvet:
Mauve mix base
White highlights
(For pastel velvets, just mix W into your base color first.)

Sheer Lace (See Page 19)
1. Make a wash of W, dab on paper towel to soak up all excess. Dry brush on to area.
2. Outline with solid W lines, dots, and any other added designs.

Wings (See Page 19)
1. Base with pale Dusty Purple mix.
2. Highlight W inner edge of flipped-over wing edge.
3. Shade top edge of wing with float of Dusty Purple mix, along complete edge behind hair, and under flipped over wing edge.
4. Make detailed feathers with W.

"Angels"

(See general instructions for face, hair, wings and velvet)

Angel Napkin Rings and Votive Candle Cups

Halo: CYM, NC — Dots.
Headband: NC and W double load side by side
Hint: Hot glue onto napkin rings and glass votive candle cup.

Bell

Float HG behind angel and Dusty Purple on other parts of bell.
Velvet around bottom: Royal Blue mix.
Lace: W.
Stripe: Gold leaf, outline W.
Ribbon: Burgundy mix and W.
Berries: Burgundy mix.
Leaves: HG and W.
Dots: Gold.
Halo: Gold, outline W.
Lace Collar: Dusty Purple, W dots and lines.
Bow: Royal Blue mix and W.
Handle: Gold top, Royal Blue middle and gold middle.

Lazy Susan Candle Holder

**Pattern in fold out*

Candle Holder: Halo CYM with W dots.
Center Angel: Burgundy velvet.
Bottom of Dress: Burgundy and W = Pink, with Burgundy stripes and outlines; W lace crosshatching and dots; Pink hearts in lace; BU shading on top portion of skirt under the lace.
Lace on Velvet: W with BU shading (float) and BU lines for wrinkles.
Ribbons and Bows: CoB and W double load side by side.
Dots on Velvet: Kim Gold mix (see page 1).
Rose: Burgundy, DP shading, W highlight; HG and W leaves.
Necklace: CoB and W double load side by side.
Little Girl's Dresses: Green velvet.
Lace: W on collars, sleeves, shoulder ruffles, scallops on bottom of dress and stripes in middle of dress.
Trims: Burgundy and W = Pink for dots on sleeves and collar, hearts, and rosebuds.
Bottom Edge of Dress: Green Velvet mix and W = Medium Green, with Green mix stripes.
Band Across Scallops: CoB and W double load side by side.
Leaves on Buds: HG and W dot in between each bud.
Shoulder Ruffle: W with Dusty Purple shading and BU gather lines.

Lazy Susan Base

Dusty Purple in center. Burgundy trim; HG on outer edge.
Center Inset: Shade DP and BU along edge of ribbon. W dots.
Lace: W, BU shading and gather lines.
Ribbon: Burgundy mix and W double load side by side.
Leaves: Green mix and W.
Roses: Burgundy mix, shade DP; highlight W; W dots (See page 20 for sample.)

Angel Candy Dish

Base: Dusty Purple.
Dress: Turquoise mix.
Lace: W; BU shading and gather lines.
Ribbon: Burgundy mix and W double load side by side.
Dots: Kim Gold mix.
Necklace: Burgundy mix and W.
Shoes: BU; with W highlights.
Trim on all Edges: Kim Gold mix.

Angel Card Holder

Base Box: Royal Blue mix, highlight across top or arch with W double loaded.
Sheer Lace: W wash with solid W dots and outlines.
Ribbon Through Lace: Burgundy and W double loaded.
All Leaves: HG and W double load side by side.
Berries: Burgundy and W double load, with W dot for highlight.
Ribbon Across Top: YO and W double load side by side.
Rose: Burgundy with DP shading, W highlights and W dots (See page 20).
Dot Flowers: Royal Blue mix with YO centers.
Graduated Dots: YO and W double load.
Clouds: W and Royal Blue mix double load side by side. (White to the outer edge).
Dots in Clouds: W — use wooden end of brush for graduated dots.
Cupcake: W paper, BS chocolate, Burgundy and W cherry.
Ribbon Candy and Candy Cane: Base in W; Burgundy strips.
Sucker and Wrapped Candy: Base in W; add a spiral stripe of Burgundy, Green or Gold.

A. B.

A. B.

Jillybean

Angel Music Box

Dress: Royal Blue mix.
Ribbon in Hair: Royal Blue mix and W.
Sheer Lace: W wash, solid W dots and lines.
Time Lace: W.
Doll Dress: Burgundy sheer lace on top.
Sashes: Burgundy and W = Pink with W wash through center areas.
Bows: Pink mix with W dots.
Pantaloons: Dusty Purple mix with W float along scallops and W dots.
Music Base: Base with Royal Blue mix. Make velvet folds with W and Blue mix.
Lace on Music Base: W wash with solid W dots and lines.
Circle Under Angel: Burgundy.
Ribbon Around Circle: Burgundy and W double load side by side.
Ribbon Woven in Lace: Burgundy and White double load.

Burgundy Angel in Center or Wreath

Cape: Burgundy, shade DP, highlight W.
Pine Needles: HG and CYM double load side by side.
Berries: Each cluster has one NC, one NC and W, and one NC and more W. Dot of W for highlight.
Wing: Base W; outline with Wash of Burgundy; shade behind hair with Burgundy Wash; Shade again closer to hair with dry brush of DP.

Blue Angel

Wings: Base W; float PhB wash on flipped edge of wing; float PhB on top edge of outer feathers; Float DP and BU wash on top edge of center feathers. Float shading of DP and BU along hair line; Outline feathers with Kim Gold mix.
Dress: Base W; shade into folds by floating combinations of washes with PhB, DP and BU. (Keep it very pale.)
Necklace: Heart NC and W – Medium Pink, with W highlight strokes; Kim Gold mix chain.
Star and Band: Kim Gold mix; outline with DP and BU.
Dots on dress: Kim Gold mix.

Angel Wreath

Dress Tops: Green Velvet mix, Burgundy mix, and Turquoise mix, were used on Angels.
Laces: W wash and solid W dots and outlines.
Ribbon Crosshatching: on bodice for some of the angels is two lighter values of original dress color. A medium value stripe one direction and a light value the opposite direction. W dots on some of the ribbons where they cross. Lighter values are achieved by adding more W to color mix.

Berries: Burgundy and W.
Leaves: HG and CYM.
Tiny Dots of baby's breath in hair = W.
Roses: Burgundy, DP shading and W highlights.
Headbands should match the dress color.
Halo: Base CYM, shade around head with orange (CYM and NC) and highlight outer edge with W. (Either float color or double load side by side.)

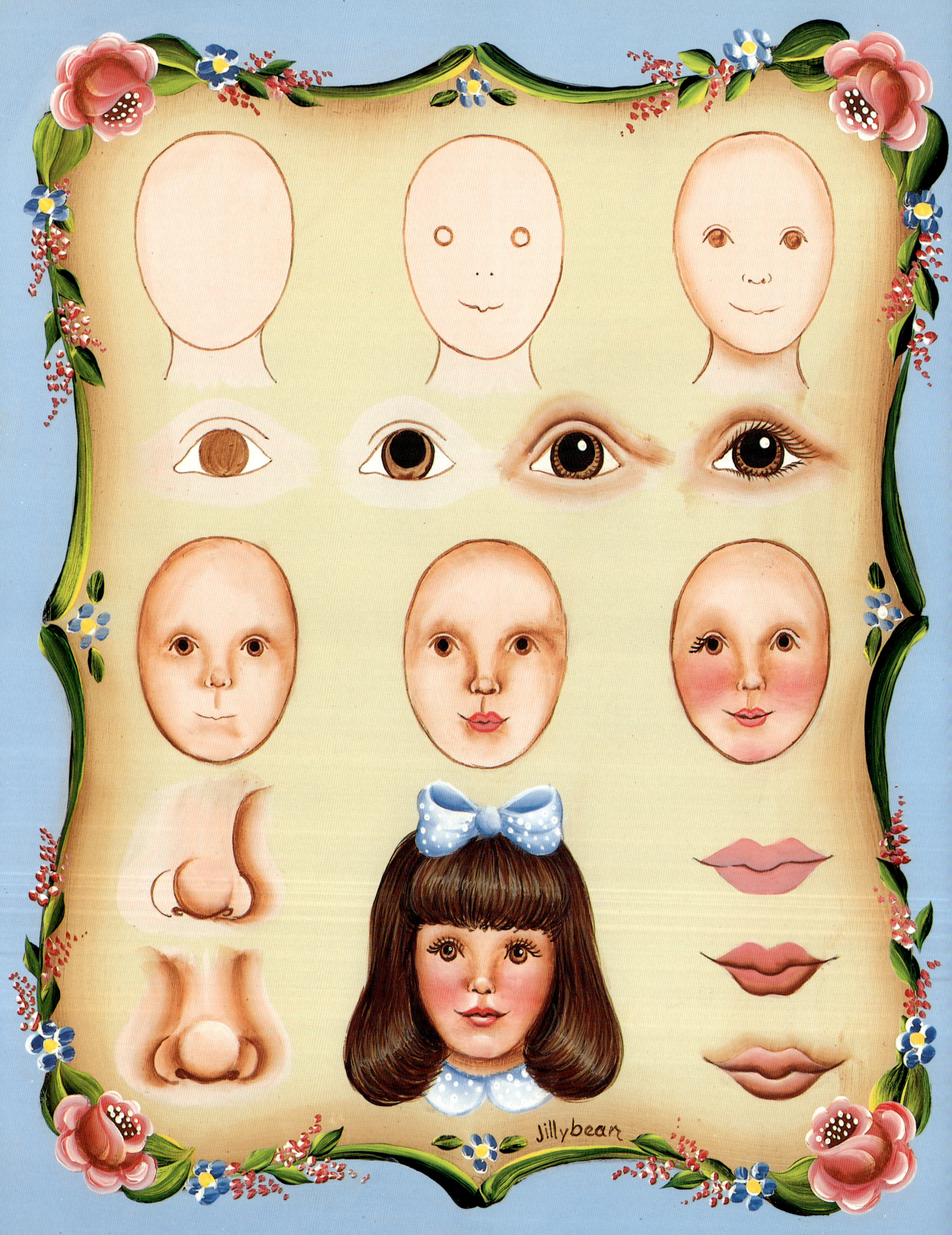
Jillybean

Jillybean

Katie
Sugar
Spice

SEASONS
GREETINGS
Tom
1986

SEASONS

Jillybean
Sleigh

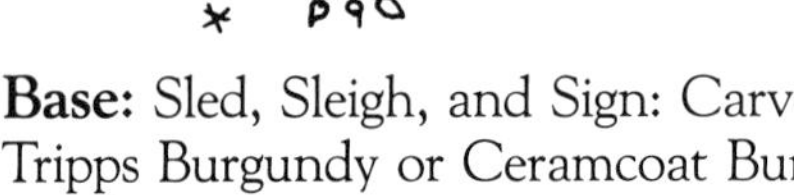

General Instructions for Skaters Series and Ornaments

(See pages 2-6 for face hair and velvet)

Base: Sled, Sleigh, and Sign: Carver Tripps Burgundy or Ceramcoat Burgundy.
Trim Edges: Deep Forest Green (Accent Country Colors).
Trace on hills and shape of inset only.
Sky: Green mix with W at horizon (double load side by side).
Top Hill: Base W, with BU and DP and double load side by side with W (White to the top of the hill).
Bottom Hill: Base W, with DP and BU and PhG and double load side by side of W. (White to the top of the hill).
Ice: HG and DP = Black. Fill in solid. While wet, add streaks of W towards bottom of ice. When dry trace on the remaining pattern.
Trees: HG Stem in middle, using a fuzzy old brush, dab on HG gently back and forth keeping branches smaller to the top. Don't clean the brush and pick up some W. Dab small amounts of W onto branches for snow.
House: RS, CYM windows, PyG outlines and door, W roof.
Church: Dusty Purple mix, CYM windows; PyG doors and outlines; W roof, Dusty Purple and more BU for cross; W outlines on cross. Snow drift across bottom of Church is W. Side load with W to the top.
Shading on Roofs: Dusty Purple mix (wash). See illustration for where to shade.
Mother's Coat: Royal Blue mix with W highlights. W buttons and scallop.
Fur: RS; shade one side of each bump of fur with BU (thin lines like hair) NC and DP lines through the center, then CYM and W lines on the other side of the bumps.
Mother's Mitten and Skates: YO; shade RS (float), highlight with W (float or double load).
Blades: PyG and W double load.
Little Girl's Coat: Burgundy; shade DP, highlight W.
Fur: W thick strokes; with W still on brush, pick up a mix of DP and BU on one side of brush. Dab shading color across bottom of all fur.
Mittens and Scarf on Little Girl: HG and W highlights. (double load side by side). W to the top. W fringe on end of scarf.
Mother's Scarf: YO double load with W to the top. Green mix and W dots and fringe.
Little Girl's Skates: W and YO = Creme; Shade BU wash on heels. PyG and W double load for blades.
Scrolls: RS; re-stroke with RS and W (See page 20). W crosshatching and dots.
Roses: Burgundy; shade DP, highlight W; W dots. (See page 20)
Leaves: Green mix and W double load side by side.
Blue Flowers: Mix UMB and W = pale blue; dab under flower area with fuzzy old brush. UMB dot flowers with YO centers.

A little boy may be stubstituted for the little girl skating with the mother. You may want to give him a Burgundy velvet jacket with YO pants shaded with RS and highlighted with W. His skates may be BS with W highlights.

Seasons Greetings Sign

Snowman: W; shade BU and DP on the bottom of each ball of snow, under hat and along edge of little girl. PyG buttons, eyes, and mouth. NC and CYM for carrot nose. PyG hat with W highlights. YO band on hat. Branches RS and W double load side by side. Scarf is Burgundy with W highlights and trim.

Snowman Sled

BS with PyG outline between boards.
BU boards under snowman.
BU and W wood grain lines and side edge.
Burgundy and W rope.

Advent Wreath with Ornaments

Take one ornament off each day before Christmas and place it on your tree. By the time you take off the last ornament, Christmas will be here and your tree will be decorated. No preparation for linen board.

Santa on Advent Wreath

(See porcelain ornament description for face)

Hat and Coat: Burgundy velvet mix; DP shading, W highlights (see page 5 for velvet).
Belt: PyG; Buckle YO with W highlights.
Fur: W thick strokes, shade with wash of DP and BU on the bottom of all fur.
Mittens: YO; with W highlights on top portions (float or double load).
Boots: PyG, W highlights on toes.
Berries in Hat: Burgundy with W dots.
Pine Needles: HG and W.
Pack of Toys: Green mix with W highlights (double load side by side).
Ball: Bottom section UMB, then CYM, NC, CYM, HG & CYM = Medium Green, and CYM.
Drum: W, NC Band, CYM Dots, UMB string; shade top of drum with BU wash (float).
Doll: Dress UMB and W = Medium blue; W sleeves, UMB outlines and dots. Face and hands is flesh mix; BU for dot eyes, mouth, nose and outline on face; cheeks are AR wash, hair is YO; RS shading, UMB headband.

Use the same
border as on the
top of the sled.
Jillybean

Velvet Stocking

Base: HG wash on area for pine needles, darker around doll and girl.
Branches: HG lines with some W lines off to one side.
Snow Flakes: W.
Beads: NC and W double load side by side.
Girl: Blonde hair, Royal Blue velvet dress with sheer lace apron. (See general instructions.) NC and W mixed for trim.
Doll: W dress with BU and DP mix outlines. NC and W ribbons, Blonde hair, BU dot eyes, HG and W leaves.

Circle Ornaments

(See face and hair — pages 2-6)

Leaves: HG and W.
Hearts: Pink (Burgundy and W).
Dot Flowers: PhB and W or Burgundy and W.
Tulip: PhB and BU, W eyebrow strokes on edges.
Rose: Burgundy, DP shading, W highlights and dots (See page 15)
Trim: Edges with color of your choice.

Little Girl Skating

Face: Flesh, AR cheeks, BU dot eyes, AC lips, BU outline for nose.
Coat: Burgundy, W highlight (See page 5).
Fur: W thick strokes, Dusty Purple float along bottom; outline BU.
Mittens and Scarf: PhB, W highlight.
Skates: PyG (black), W highlight on toes; PyG blades.
Hair: YO; RS lines for detail.
Ice: PhB and BU wash.
Scrolls: RS, re-stroke with W and RS.
Roses: Burgundy, DP shading, W dots and outline.
Leaves: HG and CYM.
Float: around outside PhB; with W dots.
Design on Sides: HG stripe, Burgundy and W dots and PhB and W ribbon.
Points: Kim Gold mix — then PhB.

Burgundy Frame

Dress and Hairbow: Turquoise velvet, W highlights.
Sheer Lace: W wash; solid W dots and outlines.
Rose: Burgundy, with W highlights and dots.
Leaves: HG and W leaves.
Buttons and Outlines: W.
Scallop: Around outer edge, float of Burgundy wash with Ivory dot in middle. (W and YO = Ivory)

Santa Face

Santa Face: Base in flesh mix; Shade BS behind eyes, across forehead, and along hairline (float). Must be done with a very light touch of the brush.
Eyes: BU wash; black pupil and W dot in pupil. BU lashes and outlines.
Nose: BU outline, shade from eye along right side of nose down to the bottom.
Cheeks: AR (float) across bottom from nose to outside of face.
Lips: AR and flesh mix; BU inside of mouth.
Beard and Mustache: Base in W thick strokes; shade with thin lines of Dusty Purple. (Ink lines on pattern are the same.)
Eyebrows: W.
Hat: Burgundy, W highlights double load side by side.
Fur: W thick strokes, Dusty Purple shading along bottom making thin lines as in beard.
Pine Needles: HG and CYM double load side by side.
Berries: One Burgundy; One Burgundy and W (Medium); and one Burgundy and more W (Light). W dot for a highlighting each berry.
Ribbon: CoB and W double load side by side. CoB dots.
Trim on Points: NC — then Kim Gold mix.
Dots on Sides: NC and CoB.

Santa with Pack

Wood Ornament

Same as Advent Wreath except toys.
Bear: RS, RS and W = Beige nose and inside ear; BU dot eyes, nose and mouth. Burgundy bow with W highlights (double load side by side).
Horn: YO, BS inside, CYM and W rim.
Package: UMB front, UMB and W side, UMB and more W top; W bow.

Becky on a Hat Box

Hair: Dark Brown; Base BS, shade BU, highlight RS, then RS and W. **Hat:** Top and bottom ruffle page Mauve mix; scallop thread on edges Mauve mix. Shade Mauve mix and BU; float wash along inner edges, solid Mauve and BU mix for gather lines. Center ruffle Mauve mix, W highlight along outer edge, BU stitching lines.

Dress: Mauve V-neck; pale Mauve ruffle (ruffle is the same as top ruffle on hat, but add pale Mauve and W (double load dot flowers). Criss-cross ribbon, double load side by side Mauve and W with BU stitching lines; W float on upper right corner of diamond shapes.

Eyebrow Strokes: RS and W double load side by side.
Roses: Mauve and W highlights.
Leaves: HG and W.
Dot Flowers: CoB and W, CYM center.
Squish Leaves: HG and W.
Sponging around outside is pale Mauve.
* Border of box shown on bottom of inside back cover.

Hair Ribbon Holder

Holder and Pegs: CoB and BU and W base, Ivory trim, Mauve outline.
Mauve Rose: HG and W leaves; HG and W eyebrow strokes; Ivory dots.
Heart: Mauve; CoB and BU and W inset; Ivory lace; Mauve dot flowers; HG and W leaves; Ivory letters.
Hair: Dark Brown.
Dress: Ivory; Mauve wash and outlines and dots; CoB and BU and W across bottom with dots, sleeves and collar CoB mix, CoB outlines; Ivory heart; Mauve outline, CoB mix ruffle and dot flower; HG and W leaves; pale Mauve bow; BU shoes.

Reflections of Becky Hatbox

Hair: Dark Brown.
Dress: Mauve.
Lace: Mauve wash pale, BU shade, W squiggles, Mauve outline scallops; CoB dot flowers; CYM centers, HG and W leaves.
Mirror: BU and W frame double load side by side; the edges are BU and W with W outlines; stand is BU with BU and W grain; BU and W edge with W outlines. Dry brush wash of W for gloss.
Washboard on Wall: RS.
Wallpaper: Pale Mauve buds and HG and W leaves (pale).
Tea Cupboard: Ivory; CoB and W trim; Mauve outlines and flowers, HG and W leaves; CoB outlines on dishes and trim edges; dishes CoB and W.
Bow: around edges is Mauve; W highlight, W gather lines, and Ivory dots.
Leaves: HG and W.
Berries: Mauve and W dot. CoB dots near berries.

Jillybean

Sugar and Spice Hat Box

Base: CoB wash on right side of inset.
Leaves: HG and W.
Apple Blossoms: Pale Mauve and W; YO centers; Mauve outlines and dots, CoB dot flowers, CYM centers; Mauve and W ribbon.
Doll: Golden Brown hair; RS, BU, YO, YO and W.

Face: Flesh mix; AR cheeks, BU outline.
Dress: CoB wash; Mauve ribbon, CoB lace edge.
Shoe: RS with BU shading.
Chair: RS; BU outline, RS and W grain lines.
Frame: HG wash in center, CoB float on outer edge; W on inner edge, CoB lace, Mauve letters and dot berries; HG and W leaves.

Heart: Pale Mauve, Mauve Shading on outer edges, W dots and letters.
Kelly: Blonde hair; CoB dot flowers and ribbon; CYM centers; W baby's breath; Dress is pale Mauve wash; Mauve outlines and gather lines; CoB lace on cuffs.

Doll Tea Cabinet

Base: Ivory.
Trim: CoB and BU and W.
Doors: Float of Blue inside scrolls.
Scrolls: RS Base: then re-stroke with a double load side by side of RS and W placing W through the middle of the first stroke.
Crosshatching in Scrolls: Mauve mix.
Leaves: Double load side by side HG and W (W to the outside).
Dot Flowers: CoB and W double load, CYM dot in center.
Squish Leaves: HG and W double load.
Roses: Mauve mix; DP shade and center; Re-stroke W and Mauve side by side load; W dots in top center.
Heart on Top Scallop: Mauve mix, eyebrow strokes on sides Mauve mix and W double load side by side; W crosshatching.
Girls on Doors: Flesh mix on face; shade BS along hair line, AR on front cheek edge.
Hair: See blonde hair.
Bow: Mauve; W highlight, DP inside bow and fold lines.

* Borders on fold out insert.

Reflection of Becky Mirror

Base: Ivory inset and lace; CoB and BU and W front around lace and down handle, Mauve stripe; Ivory back. HG wash around Becky.
Hair: Dark Brown.
Dress: Same as Reflections of Becky hat box and add white dot all over lace.
Dot Flowers: CoB and W; W centers.
Leaves: HG and W.
Border: Mauve outline on border lace; Ivory dots; medium Mauve hearts; HG and W eyebrows; on dots medium Mauve band around inset; CoB and W ribbon on band, Ivory dots.
Rose on Handle: Mauve; W baby's breath; HG and W leaves; CoB and W dot flowers.